SEA OTTERS

THE SEA MAMMAL DISCOVERY LIBRARY

Sarah Palmer

Rourke Enterprises, Inc.
Vero Beach, Florida 32964

Library of Congress Cataloging-in-Publication Data

Palmer, Sarah, 1955-
  Sea otters.

  (The Sea mammal discovery library)
  Includes index.
  Summary: Introduces that smallest of sea
mammals, the brown, furry sea otter
  1. Sea otter—Juvenile literature. [1. Sea otter   2. Otters.]
I. Title.
II. Series: Palmer, Sarah, 1955-
Sea mammal discovery library.
QL737.C25P26   1989   599.74'447-dc19   88-26442
ISBN 0-86592-361-2

Printed in the USA

TABLE OF CONTENTS

SEA OTTERS

Sea otters (*Enhydra lutris*) are the smallest sea **mammals** in the world. Sea and river otters belong to the weasel family. Sea otters and river otters look almost alike. Sea otters have thicker bodies and shorter tails than river otters. There are three kinds of sea otters but most people can't tell them apart.

Sea otters are the smallest sea mammals

HOW THEY LOOK

Sea otters are small furry creatures. Their brown coats often have a pretty silver frosting. The males are larger than the females. Males sometimes grow to nearly six feet long, nose to tail. An average female sea otter is around four feet long. Sea otters' front paws have five little fingers that they use for gripping objects. Their **hindlimbs** have developed into large flippers.

Sea otters often have silvery coats

WHERE THEY LIVE

Sea otters can be found in three areas of the world. One group lives in Southern California and Mexico. The second group lives near Alaska and the Aleutian Islands. The third group lives in the northwest Pacific Ocean close to the U.S.S.R. Sea otters spend almost all their time in the water. They are often seen floating lazily on their backs in areas of seaweed called **kelp beds**.

Sea otters are usually found in kelp beds

WHAT THEY EAT

To keep warm in the cold oceans, sea otters need to eat huge amounts of food. They eat more than one-fifth (20%) of their body weight in food each day. A fully grown male sea otter must eat about 16 pounds of fish every day. Sea otters dive deep to the ocean bottom to gather sea urchins, clams, and other shellfish or small fish. They gather the food in their right paws and tuck it under their left **forearms**. At the surface they float on their backs, passing the shellfish to their mouths with their paws.

Prickly sea urchins are a favorite food

Sea otters normally live in groups

Sea otters float on their backs to eat their food

HOW THEY EAT

Sea otters are among the few mammals that use tools. Usually they can crush sea urchins and clam shells in their strong, blunt teeth. However, sometimes the shells are too strong. Floating on its back, the sea otter rests a flat stone on its chest. Then it pounds the tough-shelled clams or mussels against the stone until they break open.

This sea otter is using a rock to break open a clam

THEIR BODIES

Sea otters' bodies are covered with thick fur that grows in layers. This fur keeps the otters warm in the cold oceans. Unlike other sea mammals, sea otters have no fat, or **blubber**, under their skin. It is very important that sea otters keep their fur in good condition. If their fur becomes damaged, sea otters will quickly lose body heat and die from the cold.

Sea otters must keep their thick fur in good condition

LIVING IN THE OCEAN

Sea otters are probably the slowest swimmers of all the sea mammals. Normally they swim at about 1½ M.P.H. Even when chased, they can only reach about 5 M.P.H. Sea otters can dive to about 180 feet, to gather food. On a normal dive, they stay underwater for a minute or a minute-and-a-half. Sea otters have been known to stay underwater for four minutes if they are chased or otherwise threatened.

Sea otters are very slow swimmers, even when chased

BABY SEA OTTERS

Female sea otters usually have one **pup** every two years. The pups are born with a woolly, light brown coat. Their adult fur begins to grow within a few weeks. The pups are less than two feet long at birth. They cannot do anything for themselves and their mothers must care for them constantly. They rest the pups on their chests to feed them and groom their fur. The pups depend on their mothers for several months.

This tiny sea otter pup has lost its mother

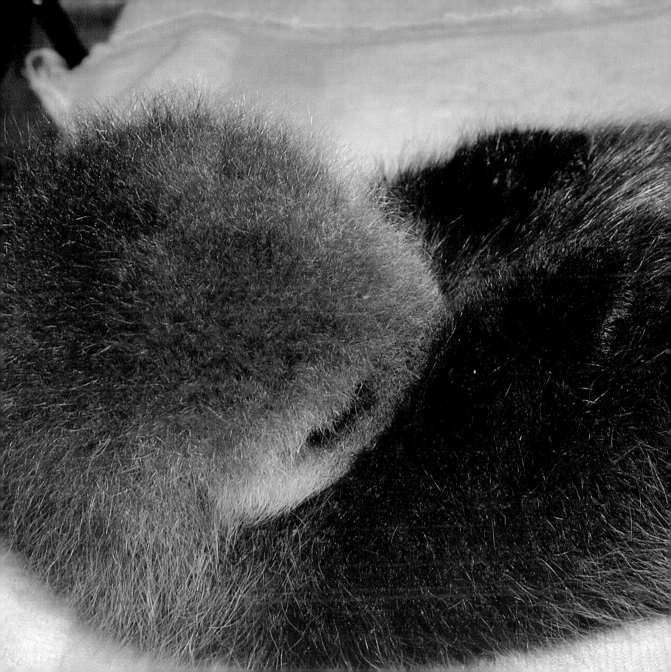

THE SEA OTTER FAMILY

Sea otters live in large groups. Studies have shown that they live together happily and rarely fight. Sea otters do not **migrate**. The groups stay very much in their own areas, not moving more than five or ten miles away. Sometimes a single sea otter will go off on his own for a while. Lone sea otters have been spotted hundreds of miles away from the nearest otter **colony**.

GLOSSARY

blubber (BLUH ber) — a thick layer of fat under the skin of a sea mammal

colony (COH luh nee) — a large group of animals of the same species

forearms (FAW AHM s) — front arms

hindlimbs (HInd LIM s) — back legs

kelp beds (KELP BED s) — large areas of seaweed

mammals (MAM uls) — animals that give birth to live young and feed them with mother's milk

migrate (MI grayt) — to move from one place to another, usually at the same time each year

pup (PUP) — a baby sea otter

INDEX